# That Book on
# **AI and Machine Learning**
## A One-Hour Intro

Jonathan Morley
Bobby Timberlake

**Thanks for reading our book!** Should you have questions, comments, or concerns, we'd enjoy hearing from you. We can be reached directly at:

authors@thatbookonAIML.com

For permissions, contact:
authors@thatbookonAIML.com

ISBN: 1793145147

ISBN-13: 9781793145147

# TABLE OF CONTENTS

INTRODUCTION                                    5

CHAPTER ONE
What is Artificial Intelligence?                7

CHAPTER TWO
What is Machine Learning?                       15

CHAPTER THREE
What is Deep Learning?                          27

CHAPTER FOUR
Division of Labor                               35

CHAPTER FIVE
Natural Language Processing                     41

CHAPTER SIX
Cars and Robotics                               47

CHAPTER SEVEN
Methods                                         57

CHAPTER EIGHT
Tools                                           71

CHAPTER NINE
Applications                                    81

CHAPTER TEN
Challenges                                      91

CONCLUSION                                      119

ADDITIONAL RESOURCES                            121

# INTRODUCTION

When we hear the terms "machine learning" and "artificial intelligence," many envision a scenario where increasingly powerful computers have been given broad discretion to make life-or-death decisions and restructure society as we know it. These scenarios ultimately end in either utopia or, more commonly, dystopia.

While we're nowhere near the "AI as overlord" scenario, we have begun delegating an increasing number of smaller decisions to machines. These may lead to unintended consequences and life-altering results. In this book, we'll explore AI's trajectory and its methods while examining some of the more speculative possibilities.

But first, allow us a bit of housekeeping. For the majority of this book, we'll abbreviate "artificial intelligence" with the letters "AI" and "machine learning" as "ML." In the first few chapters, we'll provide definitions for these and other technologies, but as a general topic, the pieces are often combined as "AI/ML" or "AIML."

The purpose of this book – like others in our series – is to act as a one-hour survey course rather than a deep dive. As such, we'll provide you with the foundation to confidently explore the AIML landscape, we'll discuss common tools being used in its implementation, and we'll speak to trends by illustrating potential future implications. By the end of this book, you'll be ready to join the conversation and contribute your thoughts. For those especially interested in related areas, we'll include varied springboards for topic-specific study and exploration.

## CHAPTER ONE
## What is Artificial Intelligence?

Most agree that the goal of artificial intelligence is to model and recreate natural human behavior. End states for these models are often termed **general AI**. General AI describes a machine with sufficient intelligence to fully mimic human decision making, and this is the starting point for such speculations about superior computer intelligence outpacing natural human capacity.

The theory behind general AI goes something like this: Once a single computer system approaches human-level intelligence, the vastly faster mechanics of computers would then allow exponential levels of self-improvement in short order. Imagine a million generations of evolution occurring in seconds or minutes – this is the very

**technological singularity** voiced by today's futurists and predicted by countless sci-fi authors over the decades. Many envision an all-knowing and omniscient machine. In the original Terminator movie, Kyle Reese's line that the computer "decided our fate in a microsecond" is the nightmare scenario, where an AI achieves near-omniscience faster than humans can imagine.

But before we go down the rabbit hole of superintelligence and its ramifications, we should note that creating general AI is viewed by even the most optimistic proponents as an extremely difficult venture. Scholarly debate exists over whether **strong AI**, as it's also known, is even possible, but there is agreement that the most advanced AI systems of today's world do not remotely approach this standard.

Instead, **narrow AI** is where significant progress has been made. Less enthusiastically known as **weak AI**, this definition decreases the scope of artificial intelligence to a singular task or a family of very closely related tasks. Weak AI results in impressive feats but only when framed in a very specific context.

Outside of these narrowly defined objectives, weak AI algorithms do not function – they're not actually "thinking." And even within the bounds of its mission, weak AI may exhibit strange edge-case behavior. We'll come back to inadvertent behaviors that can be triggered later. For now, let's keep it simple: "acting as a human would" is the starting point for our AI discussion.

From a consumer standpoint, it's easy to look at the rise of smart speakers and voice assistants such as Alexa, Cortana, and Siri as the first real AI successes. Given media attention, we might mistakenly conclude that AI progress is a recent phenomenon. Indeed, tremendous advances have been made in computer vision, natural language processing (NLP), and complex decision-making tasks, but scientists have been working to model the human brain in computing for *decades*.

There have been several periods of rapid advancement with slowdowns sprinkled throughout. Yes, the recent explosion in consumer-centric and commercially-visible use cases is a major inflection point, but it's hard to predict how long advances will continue. It's entirely possible we'll see yet another cooling period where truly hard problems (like general AI, above) remain out of reach.

It is worth noting that the bounds of AI constantly resize. Technologies that have become commonplace, such as voice and image recognition, were at one point simply aspirational markers of machine intelligence. Likewise, objectives that are now very complex to model through machine intelligence will likely be considered sad excuses for the AI title in just a few years. Larry Tesler, a computer scientist known for his technological contributions to the field over several decades, appropriately stated: "AI is what hasn't been done yet."

If you think this seems like a bit of a cop-out, you're in good company. Part of what makes "artificial intelligence" so hard to define is that we can't easily distinguish what makes true human intelligence so unique and difficult to replicate by electronic imposters. As a result, AI's journey throughout the past few decades is a tale of evolution, and this progress has followed a rather established trajectory common to most scientific endeavors. Here's how it goes:

First, large intractable problems are broken down to create much smaller ones. Next, new approaches are developed to identify solutions. Finally, the bar for what's considered unreachable is raised as previously impossible tasks become commonplace. Former dark arts, like computer comprehension of natural language in real time, are now ubiquitous in consumer-grade smart speakers. Today, for less than $20, you can interact with the AI creation formed and shaped by decades of research. Magic tricks are much less fun when you know how they work, and AI is no different. People tend to shrug off yesterday's AI miracle – the result of thousands of hours of thought by very powerful brains – as a simple and solved problem. Larry Tesler dubbed this the **AI effect**: once we get a machine to do something, it's no longer "intelligence."

We can, however, establish some differences between true AI developments and routine technological progression. Faster hardware, smarter algorithms, and new programming languages alone would not have been enough to develop the incredibly powerful AI tools we see today.

One of the major distinguishing differences between true AI and mundane technical progression is the separation of rote logic from these systems. AI attempts to provide as few rules and as little logic as possible to form its decisions. Instead of rules, massive amounts of data are used to form associations and shape the path from input to output.

A classic program for voice recognition or image recognition would require endlessly detailed rules to interpret each sound impulse transmitted or to measure each pixel in an image captured. Imagine trying to map out all the different ways a user might ask Alexa or Google about the weather, including word combinations, pronunciations, dialects, and phrases...

If these orderly, exhaustive approaches to problem solving represent the "hard logic" camp, then the more frequent alternative would be **soft computing**. This field acknowledges that some problems will be either (a) too exhaustive to logically describe or (b) too computationally intense to blindly search for one exact solution. Instead, soft computing uses various methods of best guesses, competing algorithms, and relative improvements to arrive at a "good enough" solution. For these types of problems, we don't aim for perfect: the added accuracy simply isn't worth the computational expenditure – it's good enough.

Though there are several branches we won't appraise, such as genetic algorithms and fuzzy logic, AI approaches on the whole aim to mimic the way our brains tackle complex problems by abstracting logic from solution formation. The methods are inductive rather than deductive. Instead of applying deduction in the form of a hard set of hierarchical rules, an inductive approach is created from sample input and trial-and-error. In the same way that we probably can't list out a set of specific characteristics that let us identify a dog as a dog, we've nonetheless formed thousands of associations based on exposure to a variety of dogs that let us spot Spot, even if we don't know his exact breed. The dominant set of techniques for creating and reinforcing AI associations is known as **machine learning**.

## CHAPTER TWO
### What is Machine Learning?

**Machine learning** is the set of techniques allowing a program to learn iteratively rather than relying on pre-programmed instruction from a human counterpart. That is, instead of requiring an engineer to formally encode each and every possible scenario the program may ever encounter, machine learning uses the following theory: Given a goal to optimize, a basic set of behaviors, and sufficient input data (or the ability to generate its own input data), a computer can create – and subsequently refine – its own process for properly handling new and previously unseen inputs.

Creating a model that turns inputs into outputs is certainly nothing new. In fact, computers do this by design. However, the explicitly programmed logic we're describing may be called "telling the computer what humans have already learned" or, more geekily, "human-prescribed non-learning." This is how we tend to think of computer code now: spoon-fed data and algorithms given to the machine. If A, then do B, every single time. As such, these algorithms and logic can only change with a software update.

Machine learning is very powerful because computers can iterate so much more rapidly than we can. When we fire up a new program as a blank slate, with minimal outside knowledge and only a few guidelines, the program can quickly catch-up to (and in many cases exceed) our own sophisticated (but slow) learnings.

Machine learning requires a **training phase** and a **testing phase**. The training phase builds associations and methodology. The testing phase serves as a reality check to validate the learning, with steps to correct the training and confirm the finalized logic.

In an ideal world, programmers alternate the learning and evaluation steps with purposeful frequency to ensure the machine learning model has neither drifted too far from reality nor failed to account for shifts in inputs.

To begin the process, we split our data into three categories: **training data**, **validation data**, and sets of **test data**.

## Training Data

For the training phase to complete successfully, we need to have verifiable outputs from which the computer program can learn. The computer compares its output with the expected output and then tweaks its processes until the output exactly matches the expected output. These inputs and outputs comprise the **training data**. Training data teaches the computer simulation which inputs *must* correlate with which outputs. As an example, handwritten letters might be processed as inputs and the corresponding digital text might be the provided output. This process closely resembles the way we teach our young children to identify colors and phonetically sound out words: trial and error.

We might, as an example, feed a computer millions of pictures of numbers and tell it which numbers are represented. Then, the computer starts learning by checking its output against the "correct answers" to learn how to appropriately describe the input it sees. The computer's approach to identification is largely agnostic to our exploration: We only care that it learns the correct answer.

To perform, the computer must run the data through a series of decision gates, each nudging a piece of input data one way or another. These functions are assigned weights, and the weights determine how much influence each nudge has on the final output. As the simulation progresses, the functions leading to more accurate outputs will see their weights increase, and those directing incorrect results will see decreased weights.

Let's look at an example and break down our human intuition into logical steps. To identify a printed letter on a page, we might look from the top of the shape to the bottom and ask ourselves if there are any gaps. If so, it's reasonable to assume that the letter could be an "i" or "j" because no other letters contain separated vertical elements.

The machine learning equivalent might be identification of a dark point (the dot) separated by lighter shades from a larger dark mass (the rest of the letter). Over time, we expect the associations between such vertical separations and the letters "i" and "j" to have increased weights. They're more likely to be correct. At the same time, shapes with horizontal separation ("o" and "e" and "h") may see decreased weights.

Still another set of associations for multiple dark points in a horizontal line might see weights increase for associations with F, H, L, T, Z, etc. In reality, these functions and weights would be of much finer resolution and much more nuanced, likely to the point they would make no sense to us; however, on the whole this "digital letter" example is not entirely different from the way a child learns to recognize different fonts or handwritten letters by key features, shapes, spacing, etc.

## Validation and Testing

Once we're confident that the machine has learned *something*, we then subject it to the **validation set**. This set contains inputs that the algorithm has never seen before. Because the validation set is from the original population (perhaps the same letters, just not written identically as before), we can assume its makeup is similar from a statistical standpoint (same distribution of vowels to consonants, etc.), and that anything the machine learned from the training data will apply consistently to the validation set.

In addition to validating that the underlying algorithm is correct, i.e. that the machine has learned to turn newly encountered inputs into expected outputs, the validation set is also used to tweak a model that has begun to overfit its data. Meaning, if our model has become so refined that it is coding outputs from irrelevant **noise** in the input data, the new validation data will introduce additional noise to break any invalid associations. As an added benefit, the validation data will positively reinforce existing associations.

As an example, let's examine the uncommon letter Q, whose few handwritten examples may happen to have skips from pens low on ink. This faintness can erroneously become an indicator for Q.

In contrast, common letters (like E) probably have similar examples with faintness but enough other data in the sample to average that "feature" out of the model. When we introduce new validation data with Qs that lack these quirks – or perhaps other letters with the same quirks – we catch the sampling errors in our model and allow the algorithms to correct for the overfit noise.

The final step is to evaluate the model on an entirely independent test set. This test set data is not part of the original population; rather, it is generated or gathered with requirements for a similar statistical profile but different individual samples. The key distinction from the validation data is that this new set does not help to shape the model; any persistent problems in the learning methodology will manifest, rather than letting the program simply "learn around" each new set. This input data *tests* our model's accuracy and performance.

**Sourcing Data**

The authors detail some of these datasets and their acquisition in *That Book on Big Data: A One-Hour Intro*. If you're interested in learning more about big data and its uses, you may benefit from the material in that text.

One simple method for acquiring large sets of human-verified data at low cost is to distribute simple, repeatable tasks across a large population. **CAPTCHA**s, or Completely Automated Public Turing tests to tell Computers and Humans Apart, are a ubiquitous example. A **Turing test**, named after late English mathematician Alan Turing, is a method for distinguishing humans from computers. We'll get to the irony in a moment…

Websites at risk of abuse by automated systems, such as forums, content providers, or payment processing websites, use CAPTCHAs as gates that only humans can successfully pass. It didn't take long until companies realized that these simple exercises can also be used to provide input to teach computer systems, dubbed **reCAPTCHA**.

If you've ever encountered a popup requiring you to type two words from a squiggly, distorted image, or had to identify images such as storefronts, fire hydrants, or stop signs, you were doing three things simultaneously. First, you were being tested to be sure you were human. Second, you were validating answers submitted by other humans. And third, you were providing new training data for ML algorithms. Almost certainly some of your entries are put aside for validation as well.

Initially deployed to scan and digitize old paper records, reCAPTCHA was bought and used by Google to scan millions of books for the Google Books project. Later, reCAPTCHA expanded to identify and categorize snippets from Google Maps, such as fuzzy street names or building addresses and signage.

When computers could not successfully verify the images captured from neighborhoods, humans were used to finish the work. In fact, you can use the tasks presented to guess what challenges are being tackled. Street signs, numbers, and storefronts have an obvious tie to automated mapping, and the recent shift to identifying cars, bikes, and crosswalks are likely feeding applications related to self-driving cars. What about those fire hydrants? Your guess is as good as ours.

In terms of computer vision, the old blurry text challenge fell out of favor as image recognition improved. Other variations, such as completing nursery rhymes, popped up to stymie "click farms" of human users faking social media engagement on platforms like Facebook and YouTube through likes and comments. Because these deceptive users predominately reside in low-wage countries, cultural context is used to filter relevant markets.

Another variation known as the **No CAPTCHA reCAPTCHA** simply asks users to check a box declaring they're human. Easy enough for us, but our previous engagement behavior on the web page determines whether to let us proceed without hassle or solve a challenge. That's another fun one to ponder – the systems can guess from our time spent on a website and our mouse movement whether or not we are authentic users.

From a security and authenticity perspective, this combat between humans, machines, and the human-machine systems trying to distinguish them presents an ongoing battle. But from a machine learning standpoint, every test that fails is a step forward in ML competence. You can take comfort in – or be alarmed by – the fact that you're providing input data for more advanced image recognition: You are helping the machines on their learning journey.

# CHAPTER THREE
## What is Deep Learning?


We defined artificial intelligence as an umbrella term describing computers which can imitate the decision-making process of humans. We then discussed machine learning as the practice of having computers derive their own logic from provided input without explicit instruction. The next layer is **deep learning**. We define this as a subset of machine learning in which computers iterate through multiple steps of refinement as they teach themselves increasingly complex associations between input data and results.

While AI and ML are reasonably transparent processes by comparison, deep learning deviates in that the computing system becomes a bit of a black box, with layers of association we can't directly interpret. A good metaphor here would be the links our subconscious makes without fully understanding why. Have you ever heard a song that brings back memories? How about a certain smell that reminds you of your childhood? While there's probably some logical relationship deep in our mind, we may not be able to explain what triggers a given link. If you imagine multiple layers of these associations interacting, without your ability to directly observe them, you have a good mental model for deep learning.

Early attempts to match such associations in a computer system were relatively flat and shallow. Tasking an application with recording relationships between each and every pair of pixels of an input image, for example, is insurmountably taxing from a computational standpoint. An example image depicting this scenario follows. Given infinite computing power, this approach would eventually prove successful, but the method is inherently wasteful and severely limits the power of such an algorithm in any real-world practice.

Imagine an image split into an 8x8 grid of 64 pixels (see next page). Comparing every pixel to every other pixel would require 4,032 comparisons (64 * 63). The "deep learning approach" is to introduce additional layers instead, with each layer doing less computational work than its predecessor. If we limit our first layer to the simple comparison of each pixel to the eight surrounding it, we have just 512 comparisons (8 * 8 * 8). This is a computational savings of nearly 90 percent. [For the mathematically inclined, we actually have 420 comparisons due to border and corner pixels.]

These early layers make granular associations between neighboring pixels and avoid those at distances. The premise of this layer is to associate close relationships with more significance.

The next layer in our example might compare each 3x3 block to those immediately adjacent.

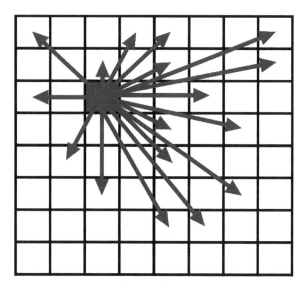

Comparing each pixel to every other pixel

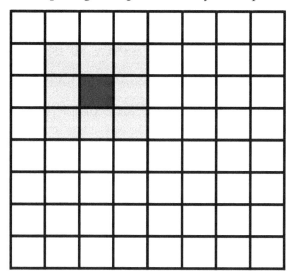

Comparing adjacent pixels only

As these patterns build into bigger features, subsequent layers can perform similar comparisons between fewer but more complex pieces.

By passing smaller amounts of data through a hierarchy of filters, we use a given technology budget (of processing power, memory availability, cloud computing cycles, etc.) in a much more targeted and powerful way. We know two pixels in the same area deserve much more scrutiny than two at opposite sides of the image, but this also holds true for neighboring lines, curves, and contours as we work our way upward and outward.

In practice, the layers are not as simplistic as the examples presented here. In fact, we typically don't have access to them in any useful form, and this is something we'll touch on later. This comparison is one good way to capture the power of deep learning's division of associations into narrow, manageable chunks. So, how can deep learning be used in the real world?

## CHAPTER FOUR
Division of Labor


The recognition that large-scale automation would not be a one-time adjustment but instead an ongoing encroachment of technology into new domains came as early as the 1930s. Taylorism, the theory of scientific management that sought to better fit workers into the processes surrounding heavy industry, yielded to **human relations theory**, a framework to recognize distinctly human interactions and dynamics as they worked with and alongside advanced technology.

Around World War II, the study of human factors began to gain traction. Broadly, researchers examined topics including best practices for safe labor, ergonomic design of tools and workstations, and intuitive design of consumer goods. For our purposes, we'll focus solely on the **functional allocation** subcategory.

Functional allocation is a discipline designed to hone the integration of people and technology. This practice asks and answers: *How do we best split work between people and technology*? This might start with a decision about whether to have skilled workers finish a part by hand versus investing in a machine to produce it.

Professor Paul Fitts, with a background in psychology and physiology, put forth a list of eleven items in 1951, five for which humans were thought to hold the upper hand and six for which contemporary machines held superiority.

This dichotomy is often referred to as **HABA / MABA**, standing for "Humans (sometimes Men) Are Better At / Machines Are Better At." Fitts' List came to serve as a reference point for future efforts to give machines human-like functionality, and is still used as a modern measuring stick.

## Fitts' List

| Humans appear to surpass present-day machines with respect to the following: | Present-day machines appear to surpass humans with respect to the following: |
|---|---|
| Ability to detect a small amount of visual or acoustic energy | Ability to respond quickly to control signals and to apply great force smoothly and precisely |
| Ability to perceive patterns of light or sound | Performance of repetitive, routine tasks |
| Improvisation and flexible procedures | Ability to store information briefly and then to erase it completely |
| Ability to store very large amounts of information for long periods and to recall relevant facts at the appropriate time | Ability to reason deductively, including computational ability |
| Ability to reason inductively | Ability to handle highly complex operations, i.e. to do many different things at once |
| Ability to exercise judgment | |

 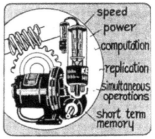

This illustration is from the original Fitts list, published in 1951.

In the right-hand column of this human vs. machine comparison, few would argue that machines have lost any ground. Humans cannot say the same. In fact, the first two entries on the left-hand side – the ability to detect a small amount of visual or acoustic energy and to perceive patterns of light and sound – have probably shifted to the machine side due mainly to advances in the engineering of sensors.

Recently, machine learning has been applied to better distinguish signal from noise. In one example, monitoring of California's Cascadia fault by Los Alamos National Lab was enhanced through self-improving algorithms applied to acoustic measurements. While sensors have a minimum threshold (called a noise floor) below which distinct signals can't be reliably distinguished, machine learning has proven capable of looking at patterns within this noise that is normally dismissed as unusable, separating the digital wheat from the chaff.

Furthering the shift in advantages from humans to machines, Google's experience with machine learning applied photo recognition and then enhancement to its development of Night Sight. Low-light photography is limited by the fact that raising the exposure beyond a certain point will introduce unacceptable noise into the image, another case where too much of the signal falls below the noise floor and is lost.

Instead, Night Sight's algorithm compares multiple images. By analyzing a set of photos taken in quick sequence, Night Sight identifies the consistent parts of the image and is able to remove much of the random noise captured in suboptimal conditions. This clever adaptation lowers the threshold of optical capture without necessitating better hardware.

Supporting the human case, Paul Fitts' items concerning improvisation, inductive reasoning, and exercising judgement are by and large out of scope for a machine, at least in constructive uses.

AI tools have been used to create movie scripts, short movie trailers, and simple music videos, but these have – at best – proved entertaining and artistic in a post-modern way (not that there's anything wrong with that).

Science does not appear any closer to generating unique, cohesive narratives or other creative compositions. Likewise, other decision-making tools, such as those for personnel decisions or moral, ethical, or utility concerns, remain limited to narrow optimization problems rather than unified strategies. While humans can always "trust their gut," machines can neither abstract nor synthesize higher meaning.

The final item on Fitts' List, storage and relevant retrieval of information, is emerging as a transitional case. In terms of quantities of data, we've seen machine explosion in the last half century, with billion-fold increases in storage density and similar reductions in cost. But the relevant recall piece has been an incredible challenge for machines to execute. Very recent developments have made headway, and we'll discuss a few.

Likely the most visible success story is IBM's Watson, tasked with interpreting *Jeopardy*'s quirkily-worded clues and then paring down its extraordinary database of information to decide on the correct answer. Later in the book we'll touch on the natural language skills that let Watson figure out what *Jeopardy*'s cryptic phrases were asking for, but suffice it to say this represented a tremendous advance in AI's abilities.

Outside of answering *Jeopardy* questions, Watson was turned loose in the medical field. Unfortunately, even after force-feeding Watson millions of medical texts, papers, and cases, IBM fell short of generating novel (much less accurate!) medical diagnoses from Watson's mountains of information.

Similar challenges exist for the smart assistants offered by Google, Amazon, Apple, and others.

Their ability to parse language has never been better, but if a user strays too far from expected requests, the assistants will default to simple web searches or ask you to try again. True contextual understanding will likely be the next major milestone for AI. While this achievement certainly represents a steep challenge, this goal is more achievable than the others remaining on the human side of Fitts List.

For the next few sections, we'll focus on some of the more concrete accomplishments of AI and ML systems, beginning with one feat that has become ubiquitous over the past two years: natural language processing.

# CHAPTER FIVE
## Natural Language Processing


In early 2018, smart speakers with built-in personal assistants sold by Amazon, Google, Apple, and others, hit the 50-million-unit sale mark. By year end, they passed 100 million. *Then*, in the first days of 2019, Amazon claimed 100 million Alexa devices *alone* had been sold. If we consider the software equivalents, included on iPhone and Android units by default, and the large number of consumers with access to an AI service capable of understanding speech, these assistants are rapidly approaching reach of the entire connected population.

This rise in voice assistant utility was made possible by advances in **Natural Language Processing**, or NLP. Unlike the automated voice *response* systems of the past – which could only parse individual words but required very specific commands to trigger limited logic – NLP focuses on turning everyday language (as spoken by a wide variety of people) into something a computer can interpret at a *contextual* level.

Processing language involves challenges relating to pacing, pronunciation, grammar, word order, foreground isolation, non-explicit pronouns, and any number of word synonyms and slang phrases. Consider something as simple as asking Alexa to "turn it down," where "it" could be loud music, the TV, a podcast, or a phone call, perhaps with several of these as applicable options but on different devices.

Before the 1980s, lack of ubiquitous personal computing meant NLP's focus was less on consumer immediacy and more on the translation and execution of large-scale works. As with other AI development, massive effort and research went into encoding complex rules and logic to parse out a sentence into discrete meaning. Of course, and as with other complex processes, both scale and utility proved incredibly difficult to achieve.

Humans are a huge source of unstructured data and attempting to apply any sensible structure tends to be a losing battle. For example, when someone asks someone else how they're doing and are met with "fine" as a response, it is a simple cognitive lift to determine if that individual is being sarcastic, dismissive, honest, or accurate. Aside from general tone, humans also have environmental considerations (Is this individual soaking wet from a thunderstorm? What about background information, such as knowledge of recent events?). Additionally, there are various personal considerations, but humans are able to determine if this is a normal response ("fine") or something out of character ("*fine*").

This is a simple illustration of a complex problem: Contextually, computers have no intuition to cover intent-driven interactions because the *intent* behind human conversation often doesn't align with the words spoken.

## From Sounds to Meaning

When a voice assistant listens to a command given by a user, a series of processes begins. The most basic of these handle the interpretation of sound by linking noises to syllable patterns which determine the actual words being spoken.

Older systems relied on exact words pronounced very similarly to inert, recorded data, but the modern use of **Hidden Markov models** (HMMs) treats voice recognition more like a reverse engineering problem. Instead of just splitting sentences at each pause in the hopes of capturing complete phrases, HMMs examine the string of individual sounds made, assigning probabilities that each sequence along the way was generated by particular words in some particular order.

HMMs use a proprietary mix of statistics and increasingly complex algorithms to label words with particular parts of speech. While many words are relatively straightforward, those with multiple uses (whether official or unofficial) will have some degree of uncertainty.

Finally, NLP examines actual grammar: how words and phrases are linked to others nearby. Voice assistants employ **semantic analysis** to figure out whether the "it" in this sentence refers to your dog, your music, or the weather, without having the subject explicitly provided.

Now, quite prominently, companies are having voice and chat bots handle entry-level questions and first-line customer support. Instead of employing resources on low-cost and low-skill support centers which often frustrate callers, companies find bot support appealing: on-demand support, at any hour, with rapid customer responses to any range of scenarios. In other words, good enough. Increasingly, support bots are tasked with gathering customer information, validating identity, and routing more complex requests to specialized teams without the need for time-consuming and often maddening human intervention. Though bots still have many limitations, when was the last time you remember hearing: "Your call is very important to us. Please stay on the line for the first available agent?"

# CHAPTER SIX
## Cars and Robotics

The evolution from fully mechanical to electromechanical, "dumb" electric, and fully computerized automotive systems has been underway, with most cars integrated across each. Throttle alone is controlled by everything from a pedal linked via cables and springs, to cruise controls using vacuum-powered cable pullers and sensors passively checking throttle angle, to "drive by wire" systems measuring pedal input and opening the throttle different amounts depending on conditions, to truly computer-controlled acceleration and cruise with no mechanical input.

This means modern cars are already making all sorts of micro-decisions for the driver, but these remain within the context of the driver's actions. In the past, simple rules-based systems and feedback loops were used, with more modern iterations incorporating large data sets. But for the most part, advanced as these systems get, they still keep you in the metaphorical driver's seat.

For this book, we define autonomous vehicles as those able to perform primary vehicular operations without the guidance or intervention of a human. This goes beyond trivial examples of computer control, such as cruise control, automatic windshield wipers, and lane detection warning systems, into a world where the computer is deciding what the car will do rather than how best to comply with your direction. In keeping with our description of AI as "something computers haven't been able to do before," these systems break new ground by being able to operate the vehicle for extended periods without a human exercising judgement or providing instruction.

## How Automated Is It?

Vehicle autonomy is commonly described using five "levels" of compounding automation.

**Level One** – Driver Assistance – describes a vehicle with simple functions but completely under the acceleration, braking, and steering control of its human counterpart. There's nothing fancy here, think plain old cruise control without adaptive functions.

**Level Two** – Partial Automation – allows for steering and handling to be offloaded to the computer. The human driver remains responsible for all critical operating factors, including environment observation. At this level, think adaptive cruise control which can slow down to match a car in the lane ahead, or lane-holding that removes the need for constant steering wheel adjustments to stay between the lines.

**Level Three** – Conditional Automation – begins to place environmental monitoring within the computer functions. Under optimal conditions, vehicles can emergency stop for immediate hazards but rely on operators to intervene in non-optimal conditions. Think mostly-automatic highway driving, with the driver stepping in only to navigate construction or traffic jams but always focused on the road for any dangerous circumstances that may arise.

**Level Four** – High Automation – places acceleration, braking, steering, and handling on the intelligent computer. Imagine programming a destination in your vehicle's GPS and waiting to arrive. At Level Four, you needn't use the turn signals, touch the steering wheel, or press the accelerator or brake pedals. To engage this level of functioning, the computer and driver must both agree that conditions are optimal for automated driving.

**Level Five** – Complete Automation – is the end goal of autonomous driving. Imagine entering a vehicle without a steering wheel, or merging onto a big-city highway during rush hour and needing to take zero corrective action. In fact, imagine not being able to take any action at all. At Level Five, the "driver" takes a backseat and the computer is the only certified driver.

Audi was the first to deliver something most would agree is truly hands-free driving (not just highway cruise) in the A8 model. In short, Audi delivered Level Three. Tesla's Autopilot mode would also be Level Three, despite initially being described as "full self-driving" and with some users treating it more like a Level Four system.

Several ventures (like Google's Waymo and GM's Cruise division) have more advanced versions, still in testing mode with human drivers to take over, and are typically restricted to ideal conditions like good weather and a specific test area for which a large amount of information has already been gathered. Within those constraints, these vehicles behave like Level Four systems, but there is still a significant challenge to be able to release such a system "in the wild" without the need for vigilant human supervision.

Aside from hoping to offer it as a consumer option on new vehicles, companies large and small are pursuing versions of automated navigation to improve fleet efficiency and safety, deliver goods faster, and even cut down on the expensive transportation of hazardous goods in heavy industry.

German auto manufacturer BMW has partnered with computer chip manufacturer Intel (and its subsidiary Mobileye) to roll out self-driving cars as early as 2021. Intel's Automated Driving Group aims to "transform the car of tomorrow into a data center on wheels," promising "new innovations and safer driving."

From a regulatory perspective, companies work tirelessly to move mountains. In the A8 example above, Audi's cars are only street-legal in Europe and can only travel autonomously up to 37 mph (60 kph). In the future, autonomous vehicles may be statistically safer than human drivers, but it is human nature to self-preserve. Because of this, a lot of reassurance – and a shift in mindset – will be required before we're comfortable conceding control to a machine. Safer on average may not be reassuring if you're the unlucky exception.

## How Do They Learn?

You might be surprised to find that AI-based self-driving cars "learn" in a very similar way to humans. As with language processing, attempts to program driving rules, exceptions, and exceptions to the exceptions proved incredibly difficult as driving is such a complex activity.

Your next guess might be that companies just programmed meanings of signs and obstacles, then unleashed the AI in a virtual setting to try things out, with punishments for hitting things or speeding, and rewards for reaching the final destination safely. But even this is too difficult, since the rules of the road are often situational.

Instead, AI was fed data from actual human drivers, effectively saying "here, watch this," like a parent to an eager, young driver-to-be. Therefore, the AI's first experience driving, like our own, is literally an attempt to mimic the average behavior of millions of drivers over billions of scenarios.

That might be difficult to wrap your head around. As humans we can't help but assign meaning and categorize experiences. Sure, you watched your parents' driving styles, but you also learned what street signs mean and to slow down when you see children because they're more likely to dart out in front of you. An AI driver doesn't know any of this; instead, it has simply drawn associations like the fact that when certain patterns hit its sensors, the average human reacts with some level of throttle, brake, or steering input. It slows down around children or dodges a car diving into its lane because of associations formed "watching" humans drive billions of miles.

At first, it may seem like this approach would stunt AI and limit it from outperforming a human. However, most instances of bad driving are the *exception* rather than a representation of systematic behavior. Lack of attentiveness, drowsiness, overreactions, and other such human error won't afflict a machine, so as long as *most* people are doing the right thing the majority of the time, a properly trained system will apply that learned behavior with perfect consistency.

These reasons are why so much real-world testing is required downstream of the training phase. A machine may be able to match or exceed most drivers with a minimal amount of training, but rare combinations of events may not occur enough in the observed data to ensure the system has trained properly for them. One measure of safety is the number of miles the car can drive before a human driver feels the need to intervene and take control, either because of a potentially dangerous situation, or just because there isn't enough data to be confident in the algorithm's behavior.

By this measure, Google's Waymo and GM's Cruise are head and shoulders above the rest, averaging over 11,000 and 5,000 miles respectively in 2018. Only a few competitors scored in the 1,000 to 2,000-mile range and the rest were well below. Uber, by comparison, scored just 0.4 miles. While there is no doubt Uber has giant databases of training data from its rideshare service, the company has received significant criticism for a handful of public accidents due to a perception that it took shortcuts on the real-world testing side.

## CHAPTER SEVEN
### Methods

Now that we've covered a few of the major AI uses, we can start formalizing the types of machine learning used in their applications. The very basis of machine learning is the ability to adapt to changing data. When designing a new system, we first must decide where the system will get its feedback.

This decision leads to one of three categories of learning: supervised, unsupervised, or reinforced.

**Supervised Learning**

Supervised learning is used for tasks that need to map new inputs to known outputs. In other words, supervised learning teaches the machine to identify new things using existing labels. There are two kinds of supervised learning, differentiated by the type of output produced.

**Classification** tasks have a discrete output. This could be a binary result, such as determining whether the picture in your iPhone matches a known face, or a categorical output, like deciding whether a picture is a person or animal. Classification tasks do not have an analog range; instead, they have a defined list of outcomes.

**Regression** is used when the output range is continuous, and these tasks use estimations to decide outcomes based on scale. Such systems might decide how much throttle to apply in a car or predict how long someone has left to live based on certain input factors. The actual number of values will be limited by the resolution of the algorithm, but the choices available can be thought of as a gradient with many shades of gray.

Whether classification or regression, both types of supervised learning require two types of inputs: the samples themselves (what is being identified), and which value, category, action, or decision is correct in each case (the outcome). Without both necessary pieces, the system has no way of knowing which pictures are humans and which are animals, no matter how many variations of each you provide.

The requirement for discrete output examples can be a drawback for large unstructured data sets. If these do not already have categorical data paired, or they use a different set of categories that won't map consistently, a good deal of manual cleanup may be required to prepare data for use.

## Unsupervised Learning

Unsupervised learning, on the other hand, relies only on samples and does not require any verified outputs. This type of learning is useful in scenarios where there are no preexisting outputs. As with supervised learning, unsupervised learning also has two major subcategories.

**Grouping** (or **clustering**) is used when there should be some type of categorization, but the category labels arise naturally from the data rather than being imposed from outside. Some examples would be finding commonalities in movies, books, or music without using existing genres, or splitting customers into behavioral groups beyond known demographics. The thinking here is to let the data speak for itself when we don't know a lot about it.

In contrast with supervised learning, we can simply use whatever relevant data sets we can find, without worrying about the existence or accuracy of outputs: The algorithm is tasked with finding those outputs.

**Dimensionality reduction** (or **feature selection**) is the other branch of unsupervised learning. This technique is useful (and sometimes essential) for large data sets with multiple dimensions. In such cases, various dimensions may not be particularly relevant but will consume tremendous computing power processing correlations. Dimensionality reduction identifies the most critical inputs impacting the output and focuses computational analysis on strictly those dimensions.

Imagine a set of customer data containing age, income, and education. Let's presume these data markers are used to predict product demand. Classical modeling would place the three variables into a three-dimensional cube. This dataset would likely be quite sparse, with clusters around correlated traits and then large empty areas representing combinations that rarely happen in the real world (say, very young consumers with very high incomes). But, if we "slice" the cube into a two-dimensional shape that captures most of the sample population, we will have a much simpler view of the relevant data and much less processing to perform.

This slicing may be simple with just a few dimensions, in which case we don't need machine learning tools. In real world scenarios, data scientists deal with hundreds of factors and potentially important dimensions. Due to scale, it's impossible to visualize only the important ones. Dimensionality reduction collapses the mathematically insignificant and selectively focuses on the pieces most important to the model.

**Reinforcement Learning**

Reinforcement learning is similar to unsupervised learning in that it does not need externally-provided labels or other answers. However, reinforcement learning goes a step further by generating its own data, typically by trying different actions and gathering information from how its environment reacts. We simply give the system a set of rewards, and perhaps punishments, along with a goal: maximize the score.

The machine begins to experiment with various actions available using simple trial and error, similar to how a young child learns a completely new skill. At machine speed, it can "learn" – that is, form links between what leads closer to the objective – and progress from amateur to expert incredibly quickly. It's important to know that the "expert" descriptor simply means the machine maximizes the score as well as an advanced user making strategic decisions can.

In a simple example, we program an algorithm to control a figure in a box. Inside the box are coins and spikes, randomly placed. We give the algorithm only three rules: (1) it can move one unit in any direction per turn, (2) its score increases when it touches a coin, and (3) its score is reduced when it touches a spike. We don't need to tell the man in the machine to "seek coins" or "avoid spikes," we just set it loose and let it wander.

In initial iterations, we would probably see the simulation stumble around randomly until it begins to associate that moves toward coins are desirable (its score increases) and those toward spikes are undesirable (its score decreases).

Adding a "cost" to each move would teach the machine to take the most direct path to each coin while dodging spikes, so long as the extra moves cost less than the movement around a given spike. If we then make each move cost more and touching spikes cost less, we might see the algorithm discover that plowing straight through spikes on the way to coins was worth the price (i.e. resulted in a higher score) versus incurring a longer, more expensive (but safe) path.

## Optimization

More complex scenarios often involve navigating uncertainty, not just for a specific action, but for a chain of future actions. If there is a probabilistic element to these choices, the algorithm may not be able to determine a single ideal path by trying every combination.

In fact, there is a specific category of problems where the user must repeatedly choose whether to apply a solution with known outputs or try something unknown in search of more information and future option potential. These challenges are called **Multi-Armed Bandit** problems, in reference to the slot machine's nickname as a "one-armed bandit."

In such scenarios, we imagine many such slot machines, some with known payouts and others we haven't yet tried. At each step we can choose to play the one we know has the best odds of those we've tried, or we can take a gamble on a new one in the hopes it offers an even better return.

This choice is called the **exploration vs. exploitation tradeoff**. The more time we spend working with a known, good solution, the less we can know about the solutions not explored. Spending time on an unknown solution has non-zero odds of finding a new optimum. The better our known solution becomes, the more expensive it becomes to experiment on alternatives that are now less likely (but still not zero) to exceed our current solutions.

Bandit problems become particularly complex when the underlying environment can change. If we spend a lot of upfront time exploring options before settling on the one that we're pretty confident is best, we can't assume our solution will remain the best. Common areas where this challenge shows up include website analytics and customer feedback: No matter how well customers responded to our website layout change last year, we need to take time to test new designs on an ongoing basis, even if we know most improvements won't outperform our already-optimized finds.

There are a variety of approaches to determining the proper ratio of exploration to exploitation, but we generally expect a diminishing return for additional exploration. That is, if we have only explored a few options, the potential value of exploring each additional sample is large, but this positive exploration return tapers off as we have lower odds of finding a better solution.

Increasing the pool of explored options also tightens up confidence intervals for future choices. In most cases, it makes sense to aggressively explore alternatives while uncertainty is high and payoffs are improving. Then, once we have a reasonable distribution of returns and see fewer cases of improvement, we shift gears and exploit the "pretty-good" solution. To ensure models don't wholeheartedly exclude new information, it's appropriate to set a floor of some minimum amount of continued exploration, especially as environments change.

## Uncertainty

We've only touched on uncertainty, which is an incredibly complex topic in its own right. However, we do want to make mention of two additional models to highlight how machine learning can tackle problems that would be intractable when searching for concrete solutions. Like the multi-armed bandit, both models fall under the umbrella of reinforcement learning.

The first is the **Probably Approximately Correct (PAC)** approach. PAC learning acknowledges the tradeoff between how accurate a result must be to be accepted as correct, and how likely that correct outcome is, computed within a limited sample size. In the simplest case, we can imagine a sequence of numbers as our sample, with a goal of predicting the next number. The longer the sample sequence, the more certain we can be in our next guess. And the larger an error we're willing to accept (say we need to be within a certain threshold of the correct value), the higher our confidence level will be. Tightening this tolerance increases the odds that we'll miss it, and thus reduces our confidence level.

The second is **online learning**, where online refers to the real-time nature of predictions. Instead of taking all available learning data as one batch, online learning operates with a continuous feed, making periodic predictions and incorporating the results of its guesses and accuracy into the next iteration.

Though it would seem the model's predictions would be less accurate, particularly early on when little data has been processed, online learning is useful when there is either too much data to handle all at once, or where we need our model to respond to new data being generated – for example, financial market data or news sentiment. Like PAC learning, online learning's output tends to be less certain; however, predictions can be powerful when data, time, or processing are constrained. PAC is powerful when we need to draw ongoing conclusions without cutting off the flow of subsequent data.

But how do we actually implement these types of learning? The next chapter will touch on some of the most prevalent tools in use, including implementations by the players contributing to their development.

# CHAPTER EIGHT
## Tools

The incumbent advantage of having huge training data sets available means that many advanced tools were developed by a handful of large firms. Luckily, many popular tools have been either open-sourced (meaning the code is available for public use, improvement, and review) or made available for free use. For tools outside of these two categories, scalable cloud computing has made the entry cost very low. In case you're interested in training a neural network or watching a computer learn, we'll follow our introduction with a few specific, free tools you can try with little more needed than an afternoon of practice.

## Initial Technologies

Many of the deep learning applications seeing success are based on a model that mimics brain behavior. A **neural network** is an architecture which uses nodes to represent biological neurons. Signals are passed from inputs, over neuron routes, to an outcome. Each step of a given path shapes the intermediate output slightly, and the learning portion consists of assigning and continually optimizing weights to these connections. The weights influence which path new inputs take and which outputs are generated as a result.

If we zoom in on one particular portion of the network and set of data, we might see the machine equivalent of how a human learns a set of tactics in chess. At any given point in a game there are several dozen possible moves a player could take. From past games, the player has built a preference for moving more powerful pieces to control the center squares of the board. When facing a new board layout not seen before, the player will scan all available moves and may override previous preference if there is an opportunity to capture a high value enemy piece or threaten the opponent's king. All else being equal, the subset of moves that put pieces in the center will have a higher priority. In other words, the brain's neural network has assigned higher weights to certain moves without locking them in as the only options.

**Convolutional neural networks** are a popular implementation of neural networks and consist of multiple distinct layers between the input and output nodes. These are referred to as **hidden layers** because their values are not directly useable. These layers represent a sort of "black box" where partial associations contribute to the overall logic but are not useful on their own.

Early attempts to build such networks involved as many connections as possible, the thinking being that more connections made a more powerful model. In a convolutional network, however, *fewer* connections through *more* layers allow for efficient use of resources, and information passes through a hierarchy of simple classifications. This network type proves very powerful for image recognition and classification.

**Generative adversarial networks** pair two neural networks with competing objectives to produce artificial photorealistic images. The generative network generates random images, with the objective of fooling a discriminative network, which in turn has the objective of correctly identifying fakes.

Like other machine learning technologies, the initial GANs faced a difficult tradeoff, with higher accuracy (more realistic fakes) created when the subject matter was narrow, and lower accuracy (easier to distinguish fakes) for a broader range of images. However, a British company called **DeepMind**, bought by Google, made significant advances in 2018 with an approach called **BigGAN**, ramping up the layers in the network as well as the number of samples available for training, producing shockingly lifelike results.

If DeepMind rings a bell, that's because it was also the creator of the **AlphaGo** and AlphaGo **Zero**, self-trained programs that beat the world's best human players in the strategy game Go.

**Mainstream Scalability**

If startup and university teams have created many of the cutting-edge prototypes that expanded the window of what's possible, Big Tech has picked up the ball and mainstreamed them. These firms now offer standardized tools that non-tech companies and end users alike can access without needing specialized knowledge, leading to several veritable household names. Each company offers a suite of cloud-based applications for distributed computations, but we'll focus on the AIML products within each.

Google's **TensorFlow**, open-sourced under the Apache license, is a set of software libraries that enable creation of neural networks on a variety of individual pieces of hardware, from the processors common in home computers to graphics cards to servers. It can also scale to parallel hardware for cloud instances, so Google offers **Tensor Processing Units (TPUs)**, specialized processors like those found in servers or graphics cards but more purpose-built for machine learning, as part of its cloud offering. This means the same projects built and tested locally can be deployed at scale without reengineering for changes in architecture.

Microsoft's **Azure** platform is similar to Google Cloud, and offers an **Azure ML** service which focuses on lifting the burden of choosing among and optimizing a variety of machine learning techniques. It is targeted more toward developers of applications that need a machine learning component, but who may not have the time and resources to devote to extensive preparation and testing. This has allowed broader adoption of machine learning as a component of other projects, beyond those whose sole focus is ML. As an anecdote, computers made a similar move decades ago when they expanded from the exclusive domain of computer engineers to tools usable by other disciplines without a huge learning curve.

IBM's **Watson** may be the name best associated with AI and machine learning in the public's mind, due to its performance on the game show *Jeopardy* in 2011. However, Watson's development has spun off a variety of services beyond the original quiz show supercomputer.

As a machine learning challenge, the tasks of parsing and answering *Jeopardy* questions, which are often cryptically phrased even for humans, was an enormous undertaking. It required natural language processing, topic categorization, and the ability to sift through large amounts of unstructured data to form a best guess at the answer. Advancements in these areas lent themselves to solving similarly ambiguous, high complexity problems such as medical diagnoses and aircraft maintenance troubleshooting, and went so wide as tax preparation.

IBM's approach with Watson has targeted corporate partnerships, acquiring new datasets and creating new learning techniques for each new type of problem. It also received mixed treatment in the media for its partnership with the MD Anderson Cancer Center, in part because of a conflict between current medical practice and Watson's approach. Medical treatments are required to be "evidence based," with backing by controlled studies, which was a component of Watson's approach but also a huge natural language processing challenge.

Another approach used, which machine learning is far better at, simply compared treatment outcomes across huge patient populations and identified any combinations that yielded better outcomes. Unfortunately, if those outcomes cannot be backed by clinical studies, they remain in the "correlation but not causation" bucket.

One more public giant is Amazon. Many readers will be familiar with **Amazon Web Services**, a suite of cloud computing tools famously initiated by two realizations: that Amazon's servers, which need to handle peak capacity during holiday rushes, sit idle most of the time, and that cheap commodity hardware applied on a massively parallel scale may prove more efficient for large computing needs than increasingly sophisticated chips and servers.

Like Google and Microsoft, Amazon's cloud computing offering expanded to include machine learning tools which are now accessible to a huge population beyond dedicated researchers. **SageMaker**, its machine learning suite, focuses on the same level of scalability provided by Amazon's cloud computing platform. Additionally, its marketplace gives users access to others' algorithms, minimizing the upfront work necessary to implement prior work. As we've seen, a common theme for the big names is to put formerly niche tools in the hands of power users and lower the barrier to entry for adopters.

Amazon goes a step further in offering certifications for its cloud services, including machine learning and several artificial intelligence tools. The certifications obviously channel users into certain tools, but they have also served to further democratize formerly academic topics.

A quick web search for any of these platforms will take you to their overview pages, but at the end of the book we've included a few direct links to get you started.

## CHAPTER NINE
Applications

While machine learning tools have received wider attention, the most visible applications have been consumer-facing. In some cases, the AI component is front and center, while in others it is hidden or just one part of the product's larger offering. We'll list a few real-world applications and link them to their underlying technologies, where possible, to show how seemingly frivolous pursuits can translate into useful end products.

**Language Analysis**

Natural language processing is an area where a positive feedback loop of learning has opened many doors. Amazon's Alexa and the Google Home smart speakers have introduced millions of consumers to artificial intelligence for basic information requests and home automation, finally crossing into territory useful enough to be worth adopting.

But the massive amount of data generated has also fed back into learning tools for automated hotlines and chat bots, letting companies shift resources from their support desks. Less visibly, ML algorithms have also powered the analysis of all kinds of unstructured text, from academic papers and write-ups of experimental data, to literature and movie script analysis.

In the former case, experimental chemists and biologists now rely on artificial intelligence to delve into published research and suggest new experiments that have never been explored. In the latter case, AI bots have been used to generate new movie scripts. So far, none have made it into the realm of high art, but they are comprehensible and expected to improve over time.

**Traffic and Routing**

Automated cars are the "killer app" that most people in the US have been exposed to, even if few actually own a car with self-driving features. But just like with smart speakers, the associated data collected from ride sharing and traffic applications has had the bigger everyday impact.

Route planning for ride services, map suggestions, and estimated arrival times have all improved notably from feeding these data into machine learning algorithms. The techniques perfected for traffic management have also been applied to shipping and other logistics, improving the global supply chain.

**Imagery**

Image recognition, drawing on massive datasets from the spambot-detecting reCAPTCHAs described earlier in this text, have allowed companies to point algorithms toward more specific applications, like facial recognition, license plate readers, and automated store checkout.

Airports and airlines are already adopting facial, fingerprint, and iris scanning for check-in processes, removing the need for boarding passes (and surely increasing odds of identifying those on No Fly Lists). License plate readers bring the promise of faster recovery of stolen vehicles and toll collection without the need to buy and mount transponders to your car. The ability to track any item a customer puts in their bag (or pocket!) while shopping has led to the opening of Amazon Go stores with a completely uninterrupted shopping experience – just don't mind the hundreds of overhead cameras and sensors.

In most Amazon Go stores, a lone employee or two handle the entire store, greeting customers and explaining how the technology works. After scanning a barcode to enter a turnstile, Go customers are free to choose items and walk out without a kiosk or line. The impact to entry-level retail jobs gets beyond the focus of this text, but closely related is the question of whether consumers will ultimately prefer the human-free experience to one which retains at least some element of the human touch.

**Games**

Game-playing machines have perhaps less obvious applications since these machines tend to be hyper-specialized. Chess is the classic example of a high-complexity game that can't be brute forced as mapping out the web of possible board positions and moves is computationally impossible for even the largest supercomputers. However, the nearly two-decade gap between when IBM's Deep Blue received worldwide attention for beating chess master Garry Kasparov in 1996, and when DeepMind's AlphaGo defeated the world's best Go players in 2015, demonstrated that far more difficult games exist.

In fact, DeepMind (now owned by Google) accomplished something significantly more difficult just a few years later when its AlphaStar AI defeated top human players in *Starcraft II*, a strategy game with thousands of options at any given time. Even more impressive, AlphaStar had an incomplete view of the opponent's position and actions during the game. This required the model to slice game decisions over time periods instead of forcing those decisions into discrete, turn-based strategies.

Though these games each required specialized approaches to tackle with AI, their lessons are being generalized and folded into unrelated applications.

This is similar to the challenge that Probably Approximately Correct learning attempts to solve. In practice, the AlphaStar AI makes heavy uses of neural networks, with a form of machine learning Google calls **relational deep reinforcement learning**. This is a subset of the category we described in Chapter Six but adds something called **relational inductive bias**. Induction is the process by which we take a limited number of anecdotal examples and form a generalized rule, the precursor to deduction, in which we apply that rule to new examples. The relational aspect means the machine tries to form rules for how objects in the game can relate, in order to create effective strategies more efficiently than through random actions. This is another example of looking to human learning mechanisms to train the algorithm.

More than just a man-vs.-machine showdown, gaming has similar challenges to other open systems like weather patterns and animal behavior. Progress in one area can open doors to advances in the others.

## Other Fun Stuff

Aside from these major uses, there are multiple smaller cases we thought worth mentioning, either as new flavors of technologies already covered or as interesting edge cases. They may not have broader, society-shaping applications (yet!), but these examples present interesting real-world scenarios.

Chinese vending machines are the first such case, where variety means much more than simply which Coke product or chip flavor is available. Seeking to differentiate themselves and make higher value products available to consumers, these companies have applied AI to predict the type of consumers who will encounter a given machine, stock novel products likely to appeal to them, let them pay with the most convenient methods possible (including biometric-linked accounts, i.e. handprint readers), and offer targeted, time-specific rewards aligned with individual behavior patterns.

In addition to fresh foods and juices, which can only be offered if they sell rapidly enough not to spoil, vending machine stocks adjust to shifts in weather and trends in demand, including such products as custom-engraved chopsticks, pet collars, and jewelry. The machines can identify new or existing customers, including those in China's extensive payment networks like Alipay, and interact with individuals before and during their purchases.

The movie *Minority Report* predicted personalized marketing by holographic representatives in 2002, and now we actually have it. Going one step further, with enough sample data from a real person, we can create new, lifelike audio and video experiences of that person that were never recorded.

The Tupac "hologram" which performed at Coachella in 2012, still the early days of the modern wave of AI improvements, involved painstaking work to generate a relatively small amount of fixed content. Fast forward to 2018 and discussions were taking place for entire simulated tours by deceased musicians, such as Whitney

Houston and Amy Winehouse, with material adaptable to each location and audience.

In 2019, deep fake videos drew attention. These realistic videos superimpose a different person's face into a pre-existing scene and are commonly used to make a celebrity or politician seem as though they made a statement someone else actually made. One viral example began with an old interview of comedian Bill Heder telling a story involving Tom Cruise and Seth Rogan. Bill's face was realistically overlaid and shifted into each character's as Bill did impressions of them. Another such fake shows Bill Heder become Arnold Schwarzenegger during an impression. This example is ironic given Arnold's role in 1987's *The Running Man* where his character is thrown into an apocalyptic gauntlet based on a deceptively-edited video. As with other technologies we've covered, it's easy to imagine worrisome interplay causing global implications in all sorts of areas: politics, marketing, etc.

# CHAPTER TEN
## Challenges

AI and machine learning have begun to perform feats that may tempt us to regard them as all-knowing, or at least capable of human-like common sense and reasoning. This would be a mistake. Of the myriad challenges waiting to trip up a team hoping to draw insights from a sophisticated system, some fall outside the "job" of an algorithm and simply reflect our desire to have the machine do the thinking. Others are problems internal to the machine learning process itself. It's important to consider both types of problems, to know which can be mitigated within the design of the system, and which cannot be corrected for but must be kept in mind as the system's output is interpreted.

**Don't Blame the Machine**

In the first category fall issues that have always been a part of any study or statistical analysis, such as blind spots and survivorship bias. One very literal case was the study of returning World War II bombers to ascertain where best to deploy a weight-constrained armor budget, by examining the types of damage returning planes took. Since only *surviving* bombers could be studied, the data set was worse than incomplete… it actively misled researchers. The damage being studied, mostly around nonessential areas of the body and wings, indicated superficial, survivable damage, while the critical areas around the engines, fuel tanks, and crew cabin seemed to take little damage. What researchers missed may now be obvious: The planes with holes in critical areas didn't return from war to be studied.

This problem can be extrapolated to studies where the outcome being measured is tied to staying in the sample. Trying to pin down factors that lead one to be a successful professional investor, athlete, or CEO, for example, must take into consideration that the unsuccessful members of the population likely move on to other things. So you may be able to show that many millionaires made huge bets in real estate or never held jobs lasting longer than a year, but you may also be neglecting large populations who did those things and went broke (meaning rather than studying millionaires for unifying traits, you would want to study the broader population as inputs to see how many had success).

The broader lesson is this: No matter how powerful, a machine learning application is only drawing associations among the data it is given. It has no ability to look outside the system, raise concerns about a lack of evidence, or identify its own limitations. "Garbage in, garbage out" holds true, but so do "not enough stuff in, garbage out" and "wrong stuff in, garbage out."

**Okay, Sometimes Blame the Machine...**

Once we recognize that any artificial intelligence is limited by what we feed it, and that we must prepare accordingly and apply our own reality check, there are still problems that can crop up in the mechanics of the process itself. Many of these issues are also inherited from the world of statistics, but these can be trickier to identify since we're typically dealing with significantly larger data sets which may lure us into complacency or make it harder to see our misstep.

All such systems face a tradeoff between **accuracy** and **precision**. The first (accuracy) measures how close our model comes to predicting true values, and the second (precision) captures how far the model wanders from the correct point. A common physical comparison made is that of throwing darts: Accuracy is your average distance from the bullseye, in any direction, while precision is how tight of a pattern you throw, even if it's consistently to one side. For this reason, the two dimensions are also called **bias** and **variance**. If you have large bias but very tight variance, you are consistently wrong (but wrong by the same amount).

Of course, we would prefer to minimize both, but in the context of machine learning each has its place as a necessary evil, and we may choose to accept more of one to grant us a better result on the other. A high bias model would be one that is less sensitive to specific training data, attempting to generalize for any number of inputs (but not being as accurate in its forecasts), while a high variance model may be overly sensitive to training data, providing a better fit to each instance but requiring major adjustments as data changes (or if the sample is particularly **noisy**).

A high bias, low variance approach may be acceptable when training data is not fully representative and changes to conditions are not expected to be dramatic. Our brains are said to work in this manner, rapidly drawing conclusions based on a few anecdotes, likely as a survival mechanism. You don't typically get to collect "big data" when being chased by scary animals, so it's better to quickly decide lions are dangerous and apply that rough heuristic to all big predators. Humans are programmed (fight or flight) to not spend time trying to decide whether bears are more or less of a threat than a lion. The risk here is one of **underfitting**, where the simple model we've created oversimplifies the causes and ignores additional data. In our underfit example, we may run away from non-predators who want to help us hunt. Better safe than sorry…

A high variance, low bias approach is one that has fewer generalized rules and might be preferred if we know our sample data to be very descriptive and robust. The reactions of this algorithm may appear to be overly sensitive, but overall, we should be consistently closer to the mark. A good use case here might be a complex system where multiple variables contribute in ways that aren't clear, like an actuary's life expectancy model. This risks overfitting, where we train our system to the specific noise in the sample – suddenly wearing green is a factor in early death alongside smoking and heart disease, because our sample happened to be taken the week of St. Patrick's Day.

**Breadth vs. Depth**

Machine learning algorithms adapt to the data provided, quickly adjusting to the level of specificity and detail. These algorithms are powerful within that given scope but fragile when a change in context is required. Humans handle context-switching much more easily; our knowledge is cumulative.

For example, a machine trained to play Go will play it very well. If the same machine is then trained on chess, it will quickly "forget" everything it "knows" about Go. That is, previously learned associations no longer achieve a positive outcome in the new game, so Go's tactics are replaced by those relevant to chess. While there have been experiments to train a machine learning algorithm in multiple games at once, they typically lack the ability to context switch. Unlike humans, who can easily compartmentalize and contextualize, a machine learning model has its budget for making associations split across very different data sets.

One suggestion might be to fully segregate the data, training, and model for each (Go, Chess), and then switch the machine back and forth depending on the task you want it to perform. While this would work in practice, we've really just created *two separate machines,* each optimized for a single game.

DeepMind's AlphaGo and AlphaGo Zero achieved wide acclaim in 2016 and 2017 for first beating the world's best human players of the strategy game Go, and then doing so completely self-trained (the Zero referencing the machine's start from scratch with no external human game data). But an arguably much bigger victory came in 2018, when a more general successor dubbed AlphaZero was able to combine mastery of Go, Chess, and a Japanese chess-style game known as Shogi.

Each of these games had existing grandmaster-level AIs who could rival or beat top ranking human players, but the ability to reach this level of play without sacrificing optimization of the other games was considered an illustrative, yet tremendous, victory. Expanding from one task to three tasks was a huge undertaking but showed that general AI is still quite far off. Perhaps an intermediate step will be a "general expert" AI, which has a categorical focus such as strategy games or legal advice, and mastery of multiple skills within that genre. A true generalist is still a long way off.

In another example, UCLA psychologists tested image recognition software to see which image features were most influential and how these processes compared to human learning. The researchers created composite images by overlaying unrelated textures on defined shapes. As examples, golf ball dimples were placed within the outline of a teapot, or argyle sock patterns were used to fill in the outline of an elephant.

The researchers found that human brains quickly recognize outlines regardless of color or texture, but the machines examined were much more fixated on the patterns – perhaps because they make up more of the samples in the image or cover a larger area of the canvas.

A similar challenge for machines can be found in the "Canine or Cuisine" images collections you may have seen on social media. These consist of a grid of alternating images with similar color schemes and patterns despite being very different content: close-ups of curly-haired labradoodles mixed in with fried chicken, sheepdogs and mops, corgis and bread loaves, etc.

Sure, humans often confuse them at a quick glance, but we also immediately double-take and re-classify the images correctly. We easily shift focus from the broad pattern and color scheme to specific markers or details that let us recognize a Shar-Pei puppy from a folded towel. Machines, on the other hand, apply the same model built from their samples, so there is no recognition of anything unusual, no change in focus (from "recognize every object we've ever seen" to "tell dalmatians and ice cream apart"), and therefore no hunt for finer details.

The lack of simply *knowing* to look more closely makes all kinds of identification difficult for a general image recognition algorithm. Again, the algorithm could be retrained on a new sample of images to distinguish between corgis and bread loaves, but this would come at the cost of being able to recognize every other object it encounters. As in our Go vs. Chess example, a machine trained on both general image recognition *and* puppy vs.

bagel comparisons would demonstrate its effectiveness plunge as the neural network fragmented across countless comparisons.

Just for fun, we've included a handful of these collages at the end of the chapter...

**More Intelligence, More Problems**

Often researchers find themselves in a space where the intermediate machine processing isn't decipherable to human eyes or logic. In a slightly comical (yet true) example, Facebook ended a machine learning trial where the output was no longer understandable by the researchers themselves. Tasked with negotiation exercises, the computer simulation had developed its own shorthand, exchanging information that looked like gibberish, and we presume the developers weren't comfortable not knowing what the computer was keeping secret.

This particular scenario was benign, but one can imagine the concerns as we place more critical systems under AI control. And there are ethical and social considerations... What do we do when a computer becomes "smarter" than the people who programmed it, or the decisions being made do not conform with common social constructs? If an autopilot takes the plane into a sudden steep bank or dive, will we be able to distinguish superhuman evasive action from a life-ending error in logic?

Back in the present, there exists a very popular machine learning work in which a computer learns to play Super Mario World. Seth Bling, the engineer behind "MarI/O," (I/O being a common shortening of input/output) tells the computer that the score (or *fitness*) increases as Mario moves to the right, horizontally, across the screen. Bling also tells the computer that a higher score is the primary objective to be maximized.

Subject to just these constraints, MarI/O repeatedly generated random neural networks connecting what it observed in the level (safe land and platforms, inbound threats) and which buttons it could press in response. In just 34 machine learning generations, a simple neural network was discovered that could complete the first level of the game without a tragic Mario death. Over 24 hours, various successful networks were mixed and matched – for example, some simply ran to the right and jumped only when necessary, others jumped nonstop to maximize odds of dodging ground-based enemies, etc.

The end result was a much more complex neural network that had evolved to incorporate multiple tactics not unlike a skilled human player. This network was general enough to quickly conquer new levels it had never seen. While impressive and entertaining, consider that Super Mario only has eight possible inputs across two degrees of freedom: up, down, left, right, and the A, B, X, Y buttons.

**The Three Ds**

Game challenges aside, there are other more pressing challenges that will become increasingly important as AI advances. Concerns over job loss due to robotic automation have received increasing attention the past few years. While much of this is on the physical side, there is a strong software component that is worthy of mention, particularly for readers trying to assess what career paths may recede and which ones may expand.

The classic focus for automation is jobs which can be described as **dirty, dangerous, and demeaning**. Examples include many jobs that take place in harsh conditions, use heavy machinery, or involve repetitive work where errors lead to injury. Mining and extraction, crop planting and harvesting, roofing, construction, trucking, and underwater welding are great examples.

At first glance, these jobs have traits which make them less appealing to humans and present the most likely areas for efficiency through automation. On the other hand, such roles often have lower barriers of entry and, for those unbothered by such conditions, these roles can result in very good wages. For these, any shift to robotics would be economically disruptive.

For our purposes, it makes sense to distinguish jobs which are simply physically difficult and dangerous, but still require dexterity and flexibility a physical machine can't yet provide, from those which also require human judgement and contextual decision-making skills. The latter are typically viewed as more automation-resistant but will increasingly come into scope as AI and machine learning systems advance.

As such, for the reader looking for answers on which careers may be threatened, we would start by assessing the degree to which the work is rule- or process-bound and where performance could be improved by a worker with access to a library of information or historical data. So, an airline mechanic whose value comes from their intuition of which expensive aerospace component should be replaced to get an engine working again will likely find themselves either using or competing with AI diagnostic software which has been fed an unmatched library of maintenance data.

Jobs requiring some level of creativity or inventiveness are often described as being "safe" from automation, but we think a better focus is on the degree of freedom for decision-making and measurability of outcomes. As we've seen, AI is much more difficult when the range of decisions is not discrete and when it's hard to link a given action to the outcome being optimized, such as complex business strategies and the subsequent company earnings that have any number of outside contributing factors.

In our airline mechanic example, the machinist able to tool up for a one-off job whose needs are unique and for which downtime is very expensive will be more resilient to automation than someone involved in more routine production whose efficiency can be surpassed by a sufficiently well-trained machine.

# Labradoodle or Fried Chicken?

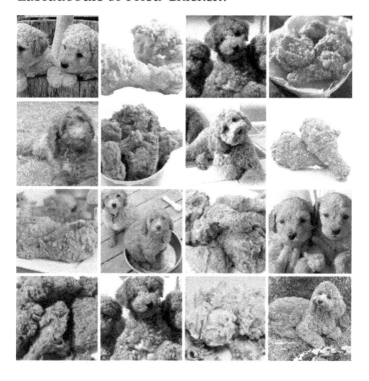

# Dalmatian or Ice Cream?

# Sheepdog or Mop?

# Puppy or Chocolate?

# CONCLUSION

We hope you've enjoyed *That Book on AI and Machine Learning*. We've done our best to touch on the key topics in a constantly-evolving field.

Based on feedback from our prior publications, we've expanded our vocabulary list. Most terms that follow were mentioned in the text, but we've added a few others you may find interesting. We've also included some of the viewpoints and articles that shaped this book. If you'd like to continue learning, we think these are great springboards.

Finally, we'd love your input. You can leave us feedback on our Amazon page or reach out directly by email: authors@thatbookonAIML.com

Thank you for learning with us. If you enjoyed it, we'd encourage you to read others in the series.

Take care!

# ADDITIONAL RESOURCES

## Articles and Whitepapers

AI vs. Machine Learning vs. Deep Learning.
  Skymind.
  https://skymind.ai/wiki/ai-vs-machine-
  learning-vs-deep-learning

Amazon Echo, Google Home Installed Base Hits 50
  Million; Apple has 6% Market Share. John
  Koetsier, Forbes.
  https://www.forbes.com/sites/johnkoetsier/2
  018/08/02/amazon-echo-google-home-
  installed-base-hits-50-million-apple-has-6-
  market-share-report-says

Can Artificial Intelligence Tell a Teapot from a
  Golf Ball? Science Daily. 7 January 2019.
  https://www.sciencedaily.com/releases/2019
  /01/190107131236.htm

Deal or No Deal? Training AI Bots to Negotiate.
  Facebook Code, 14 June 2017.
  https://code.fb.com/ml-applications/deal-or-
  no-deal-training-ai-bots-to-negotiate/

DeepMind's Go Playing Software Can Now Beat
  You at Two More Games. New Scientist. 6
  December 2018.

https://www.newscientist.com/article/2187599-deepminds-go-playing-software-can-now-beat-you-at-two-more-games/

Doodle or Chicken? Bark Post. https://barkpost.com/humor/doodle-or-fried-chicken-twitter/

In China, Lowly Vending Machines are Transforming into Smart Storefronts. Digital Trends. Joshua Bateman. 23 March 2018. https://www.digitaltrends.com/business/how-china-is-revitalizing-the-vending-machine/

Is This Photo Real? AI Gets Better at Faking Images. Tom Simonite, WIRED Magazine. https://www.wired.com/story/is-this-photo-real-ai-getting-better-faking-images/

Machine Learning-Detected Signal Predicts Time to Earthquake. Nancy Ambrosiano, Los Alamos National Laboratory. https://phys.org/news/2018-12-machine-learning-detected-earthquake.html

MarI/O. Jason Kottke. 15 June 2015. https://kottke.org/15/06/mario

MD Anderson Benches IBM Watson in Setback for Artificial Intelligence in Medicine. Matthew Harper, Forbes. https://www.forbes.com/sites/matthewherper/2017/02/19/md-anderson-benches-ibm-watson-in-setback-for-artificial-intelligence-in-medicine

P.M. Fitts, "Human Engineering for an Effective Air Navigation and Traffic Control System," tech. report, Nat'l Research Council, 1951.

The Self Driving Car Companies Going the Distance. PC Mag. Rob Marvin. 1 March 2019. https://www.pcmag.com/article/366797/which-self-driving-cars-put-in-the-most-fully-autonomous-mil

Unprovability Comes to Machine Learning. Nature, Lev Reyzin. 7 January 2019. https://www.nature.com/articles/d41586-019-00012-4

Where Machines Could Replace Humans – and Where They Can't (Yet). McKinsey Quarterly. July 2016. https://www.mckinsey.com/business-functions/digital-mckinsey/our-insights/where-machines-could-replace-humans-and-where-they-cant-yet

Why the Fitts List Has Persisted Throughout the History of Function Allocation. JCF de Winter, D Dodou. 25 August 2011. https://link.springer.com/article/10.1007/s10111-011-0188-1

## Tools to Try

Tensor Flow Playground – interactive browser-based tool, no setup required https://playground.tensorflow.org/

Tensor Flow Neural Network – some coding required, but still beginner level https://www.tensorflow.org/tutorials/keras/basic_classification

Tensor Flow Generational Adversarial Network – for more advanced users https://www.tensorflow.org/alpha/tutorials/generative/dcgan

PyTorch – an open-source Python library for natural language processing https://pytorch.org/

Google AI – sample data sets https://ai.google/tools/#datasets

IBM Watson – tone analysis demo
https://natural-language-understanding-demo.ng.bluemix.net/

Jobscan AI – job description resume-optimizer
https://www.jobscan.co/

# VOCABULARY

**Artificial Intelligence** – technology which mimics human behavior or decision-making. Informally, computer replication of human actions beyond whatever is currently achievable

**AI Effect** – Larry Tesler's phrase describing the phenomenon where AI achievements are dismissed as not being "true" intelligence; continually redefining AI as anything that has not yet been solved

**AI Winter** – periods from the 1970s through 1990s leading to collapses in funding and research during which key artificial intelligence technologies failed to advance sufficiently or deliver on initial expectations

**Bias** – a measure of the expected overall error between predicted and actual values, often in the context of supervised machine learning

**CAPTCHA** – Completely Automated Public Turing test to tell Computers and Humans Apart. A test ("easy on humans, hard on bots") whereby users are given text, picture, or audio and prompted to type or select content to prove they are humans, often to prevent abuse by automated scripts

**Cluster Analysis** – the practice of examining data in dimensions for grouping without predefined division points

**Coffee Test** – a lesser known variant of the Turing test proposed by Steve Wozniak, whereby a robot would be asked to navigate a typical house, find the ingredients, and successfully brew a cup of coffee with unfamiliar equipment

**Convolutional Neural Network** – a highly optimized form of neural network, using more layers with narrower connections to process the most relevant data (such as neighboring pixels in a photo but not those far away) and minimize manual data processing

**Deep Learning** – a field of iterative machine learning where data passes through multiple layers of evaluation and feedback is used to repeatedly refine the model

**Dirty, Dangerous, and Demeaning** – sometimes shortened to the 3Ds, a concept encapsulating work that is undesirable across several dimensions of comfort

**Exploitation** – in the context of reinforcement learning, the portion of effort devoted to maximizing output through pathways with known performance or probabilities

**Exploration** – in the context of reinforcement learning, the portion of effort devoted to searching new pathways with unknown outputs

**Fitts' List** – a list of 11 items put forth in 1951 by Paul Fitts, separating key work functions into those better performed by machines and those better performed by humans

**Functional Allocation** – a subset of human factors devoted to determining whether a given task is better performed by a person, an automated system, or a person with the assistance of a tool or technology

**General AI** – artificial intelligence capable of completing a broad set of tasks on par with human abilities; not currently feasible, some debate as to whether ever feasible.

**Generative Adversarial Network** – a neural network, typically one half of a pair, assigned to either generate new content or judge whether content is natural or computer-generated

**GOFAI** – Good Old-Fashioned AI, another name for Symbolic AI that attempted to encode high-level logic using fixed rules

**HABA / MABA** – Humans Are Better At / Machines Are Better At, a comparison of skills where each was thought to have the edge

**Hidden Markov Model** – in the context of language processing, the step in which individual sounds are combined into probable words (see Semantic Analysis)

**Human Factors** – a field of study concerning the interaction between people and systems or tools

**Human Relations Theory** – a field of study exploring the higher level social and psychological components of workers as they performed their job functions

**Machine Learning** – a field of computer science in which input data drives an output algorithm through multiple iterations rather than externally provided rules

**Multi-Armed Bandit** – a class of problems surrounding the optimum allocation of effort between the exploration of new techniques with unknown payouts and the exploitation of methods with known payouts

**Narrow AI** – artificial intelligence developed for a specific use case, such as text analysis or a chess-playing robot

**Natural Language Processing** – a branch of artificial intelligence focused on parsing human language as it is naturally expressed, for example handling different word order, synonyms, slang, or partially captured sentences

**Neural Network** – a tool associated with deep learning in which nodes and connections are modeled on biological neurons and synapses and data is used to create associations between nodes and their connections

**Noise** – extraneous data that can cause confusion to machine learning algorithms

**Online Learning** – also online machine learning, an approach that incorporates individual data samples in sequence, issuing predictions and incorporating the outcome in real-time (see Probably Approximately Correct Learning)

**Overfitting** – an undesirable machine learning outcome whereby the model incorporates too much detail, reading random noise as signal

**Precision** – a measure of how much an estimate can be expected to wander from the true value as new data is introduced

**Probably Approximately Correct Learning** – a machine learning approach that recognizes the tradeoff between the accuracy of a model, and the likelihood that it is correct, for a given quantity of sample data (see Online Learning)

**reCAPTCHA** – a refinement of CAPTCHA tests to determine users of a system are human, using pairs of words scanned from paper books and articles, where one is known (the test) and the other is not

**Reinforcement Learning** – a branch of machine learning in which maximizing an objective function through a balance of the exploration and exploitation

**Relational Inductive Bias** – a machine learning technique that attempts to create generalized rules from anecdotal data (induction), with an emphasis on how objects relate to one another

**Semantic Analysis** – in language processing, the step after individual words are identified in which phrase structure is interpreted (see Hidden Markov Models)

**Soft Computing** – a branch of computing that applies various best-guess approaches to problems too complex to solve exhaustively

**Strong AI** – another term for General AI

**Structured Data** – data entries that fit nicely within a set of static rows and columns

**Supervised Learning** – a class of machine learning where labeled training data is required, typically for tasks where categories are already defined

**Symbolic AI** – an early approach to AI that attempted to code high-level logic into machines, proving successful for very ordered tasks but facing challenges with nuanced or less predictable ones (see GOFAI)

**Technological Singularity** – the point at which a sufficiently intelligent machine is able to teach itself at increasing rates, far surpassing any human intellectual capabilities

**Test Set** – data gathered or generated separately from the initial sample used in machine learning training, solely to evaluate performance without changing the model (see Training Set, Validation Set)

**Training Set** – data provided as input for a machine learning system and used to generate the initial model (see Validation Set, Test Set)

**Turing Test** – created by computer scientist Alan Turing, a generalized test of whether a machine can generate responses or output indistinguishable from those of a human

**Underfitting** – an undesirable machine learning outcome whereby the model remains overly general, failing to capture associations in the test data

**Unstructured Data** – data that does not fit a consistent layout, often unordered text generated by human input

**Unsupervised Learning** – a class of machine learning where data is input with no need for labels, typically for tasks where output categories either do not exist or are unknown

**Validation Set** – data held back from the initial population of a machine learning sample set and used to tweak the initial model and avoid overfitting (see Training Set, Test Set)

**Weak AI** – another term for Narrow AI